I0800588

FUN with the ACCORDION

Fun With the Accordian is a collection of easy solos in varying styles of music. Polkas, Ragtime, Bluegrass, Dixieland, and Songs From Many Lands are included. All of the selections were carefully arranged to provide a full accordian sound. We hope this book will give you many hours of musical Fun and Enjoyment!

MEL BAY®

WWW.MELBAY.COM

CONTENTS

Hatikvoh

Hebrew National Anthem

Hava Nagila

Lively Hebrew Dance

Organ Style Bass

Children's Song

Spanish Dance

Not too fast

Alouette

French Canadian

Moderately

San Francisco Here I Come

D Maj
A7
D
D
G
G F♯ E D
G
M
G
D7
7
G F♯ E D
G
M
G
E7
7
A mi
mi
C
C
C♯
M
A mi
mi
D7
7
G
G

Ride Ranger Ride

Gypsy Dance

V. Herbert

The Entertainer

Not too fast

Scott Joplin

Santa Lucia

Neopolition Song

The Stars And Stripes Forever

Lively

Sausa

Come Back To Torino

Francesco Carlo Zucco

Moderato

Dixie

Brightly
C F F C
M 4 M
C G7 C F
3 7 M 3
C G7 C
7
F D7 G7 C F C
7 7
G7 C G7 C G7 C C
7 7 7

Flop Eared Mule

Blue Grass

Just A Closer Walk With Thee

Moderately

Spiritual

We Wish You A Merry Christmas

Careless Love Boogie

Tempo boogie

Soul Song

Allegretto

Bach

Gold And Silver

Strauss

Tempo di waltz

Sweet Molly Malone

Singing style

Dark Eyes

Ala gypsy

Gypsy Song

Streets Of Larredo

Moderato

Cowboy Song

Now The Day Is Over

Hymn

Joy

Beethoven

Andante

Down In The Valley

Waltz time

Traditional

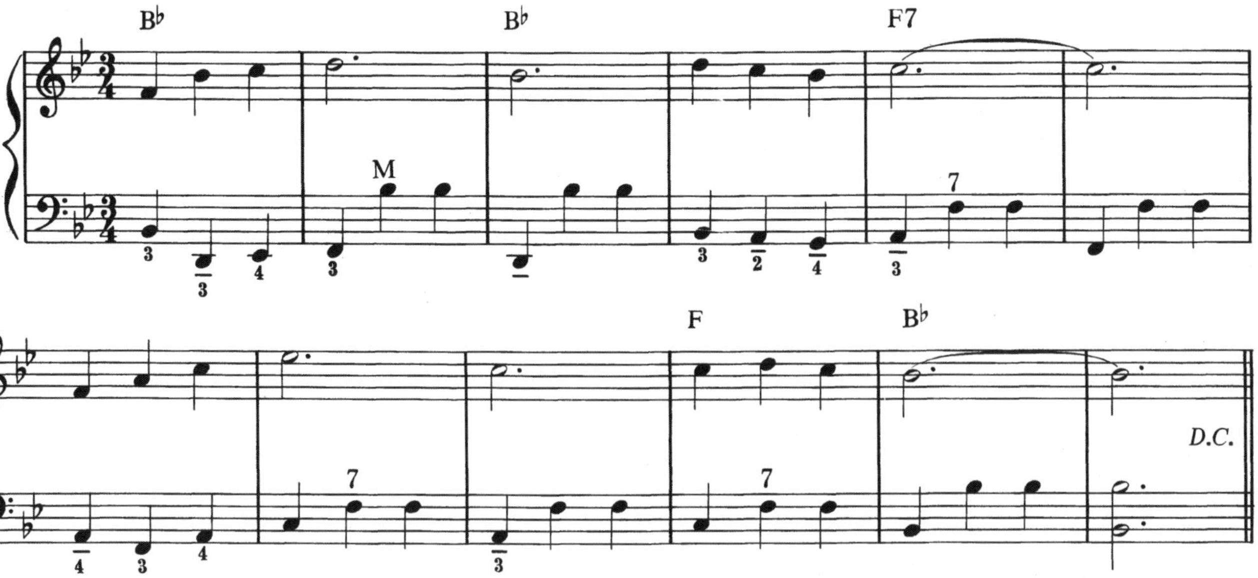

Kum-Ba-Ya

Slowly
C
F
C
G7
M
M
M
C
G7
G7
F
G7
C
F
C
G7
3
Bass Solo
2
C
F
C
G7
G7
C
4

When The Saints Go Marching In

Spiritual

With a beat

Medley: Aura Lee And Loch Lomond

Big Mama

Polka tempo

Siro Teck

Traditional

Jenny Lind Polka

Not too fast